Contents

KU-015-270

Any words appearing in the text in bold, **like this,** are explained in the glossary. You can also look out for them in the Word Bank box at the bottom of each page.

Where in the world?

National dress

The national dress for Vietnam is the *Ao dai* – a beautiful long tunic worn over a pair of large trousers. Girls usually wear a white *Ao dai*, a symbol of purity. Young, unmarried women tend to wear softer shades. Only married women wear dark, rich colours.

You are snapped out of your daydream by loud clanging. You run outside and find hundreds of children parading through the streets, banging drums, gongs, and other instruments. Unicorns and dragons dance through the crowds, and many people are carrying candle-lit lanterns. A girl wearing a tiger mask and an *Ao dai* pounces in front of you. She says you have arrived at the perfect time, as everyone is celebrating *Tet Trung Thu* – the Mid-Autumn Festival. This festival is also known as the Children's Festival.

The Mid-Autumn Festival is celebrated in September or October, when there is a full moon. Children dress up in masks and carry lanterns.

Vietnamese population

Vietnam is quite small – about the same size as New Mexico in the United States. But Vietnam is home to almost 83.5 million people, while New Mexico only has around 1.8 million!

There are toy stalls everywhere, and lots of parents are giving their children handfuls of money to buy lanterns and candles. You have a look at one of the notes – on it there is a picture of Ho Chi Minh and the name of the currency: Vietnam dong (VND). You've got it! You're in Ho Chi Minh City – the largest city in Vietnam!

Sweet moon-cakes, usually filled with egg or seeds, are a popular gift during the Mid-Autumn Festival.

Find out later...

What important crop are these people planting?

Where can you find markets on water?

Which is the longest river in Vietnam?

So this is Vietnam

You pop into a street café and grab a baguette for breakfast. The smell of fresh coffee wafts through the room. A piece of scrunched-up paper is lying on the table. You open it up and realize it's a map of Vietnam, with some notes scribbled on it. This should help!

The Mekong Delta is a beautiful, tropical region where most of Vietnam's rice comes from.

Hanoi, Vietnam's capital, is an ancient city, filled with old buildings.

The Vietnamese year
There are only 355 days in a normal Vietnamese year! Vietnam uses a **lunar calendar**, which has twelve months of 29 or 20 days each. Every third year, an extra month is included between the third and fourth months.

WORD BANK   Communism belief that all the wealth created by industry should be shared amongst everyone in society

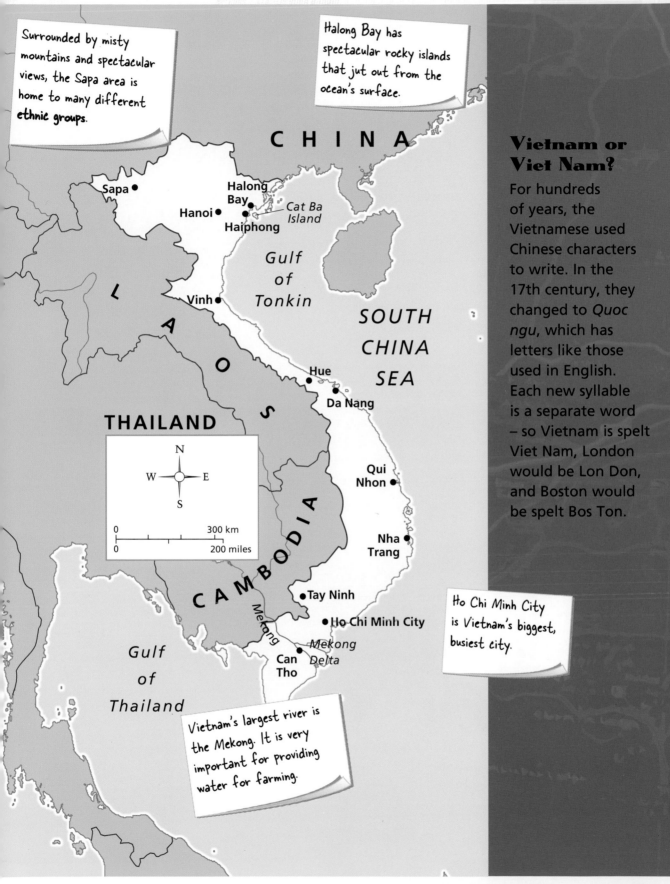

Surrounded by misty mountains and spectacular views, the Sapa area is home to many different **ethnic groups**.

Halong Bay has spectacular rocky islands that jut out from the ocean's surface.

C H I N A

Sapa •

Halong Bay •
Hanoi • • — Cat Ba Island
Haiphong •

Gulf of Tonkin

Vinh •

SOUTH CHINA SEA

L A O S

THAILAND

N
W ○ E
S

0   300 km
0   200 miles

Hue •
Da Nang •

Qui Nhon •

Nha Trang •

C A M B O D I A

Tay Ninh •
• Ho Chi Minh City
Mekong Delta
Can Tho •

Mekong

Gulf of Thailand

Vietnam's largest river is the Mekong. It is very important for providing water for farming.

Ho Chi Minh City is Vietnam's biggest, busiest city.

Vietnam or Viet Nam?

For hundreds of years, the Vietnamese used Chinese characters to write. In the 17th century, they changed to *Quoc ngu*, which has letters like those used in English. Each new syllable is a separate word – so Vietnam is spelt Viet Nam, London would be Lon Don, and Boston would be spelt Bos Ton.

ethnic group people who share a culture or nationality
lunar calendar calendar based on the cycle of the moon

7

Everyday life

Study hard

Vietnamese children study mathematics, history, science, geography, art, music, and Vietnamese. In secondary school, students usually study English. Learning how to read and write is considered to be very important.

You get up early the next morning and see lots of children cycling to school. They look very smart in their school uniforms. You ask one of the girls what it's like going to school in Vietnam. She explains that students go to school for half a day, either in the morning or in the afternoon. The schools have to do this because there are so many children that there is not enough space to fit everyone in for the whole day.

Classrooms have very little equipment – just desks and chairs for the students and a blackboard for the teacher. However, they are often decorated with flowers and pictures.

WORD BANK rural relating to the countryside

Vietnamese schools

Most schools have lots of students and few facilities. Vietnamese students study very hard, as they know education is very important if they are to get on in life. Elementary students go to school five days a week. Middle and High School students go to school six days a week. When they are not studying, they help their families with work and chores. There is a long summer break from June to September, so that children in **rural** areas can help with the annual rice harvest.

Children make up 41 percent of Vietnam's population – that's over 34 million children!

Teachers' Day

Children in Vietnam have a lot of respect for their teachers – so much so that on 20 November everyone celebrates "Teachers' Day". On this day, students visit their current and former teachers, and give them gifts like flowers.

9

Religion in Vietnam

The main religion in Vietnam is Buddhism. Most people who follow Buddhism, are Mahayana Buddhists. The religion was founded in India in the 6th century BC, and spread to Vietnam 800 years later. Most Buddhists worship in a **pagoda**.

Buddhists believe that there is a cycle of birth, life, death, and **reincarnation** – which means that when you die you are reborn. They also believe in karma, where every cause has an effect. This means that when you die, good behaviour is rewarded in the afterlife and bad behaviour is punished – similar to the saying, "What goes around comes around".

Confucianism

Confucianism is extremely important in Vietnam. It is not really a religion, more a set of rules about how to live a good life. In particular, Confucianism stresses the importance of being respectful to elders – a custom you can see throughout the country.

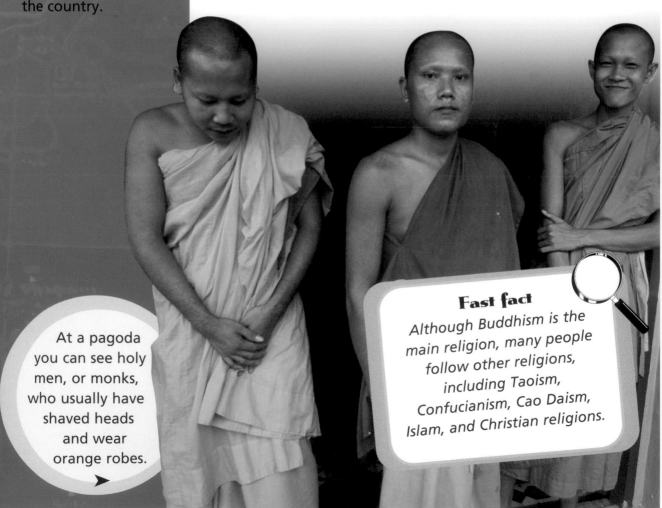

At a pagoda you can see holy men, or monks, who usually have shaved heads and wear orange robes. ▶

Fast fact
Although Buddhism is the main religion, many people follow other religions, including Taoism, Confucianism, Cao Daism, Islam, and Christian religions.

WORD BANK   pagoda T-shaped building, with a bell-tower, used for worship
reincarnation belief that a person will be reborn after they die

Cao Daism

Three million Vietnamese people follow Cao Daism – a mixture of Confucianism, Christianity, Buddhism, Islam, and Taoism. The Cao Dai temple at Tay Ninh has become a tourist attraction. It is so colourful that it looks more like a fun park than a religious monument! Inside, is a kaleidoscope of colour – paintings of clouds and stars cover the roof and big *nagas*, or snakes, cover large columns.

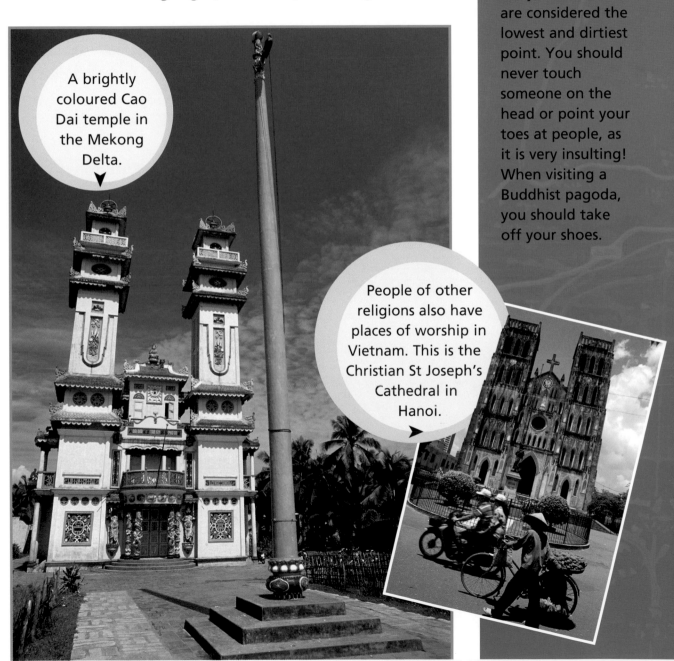

A brightly coloured Cao Dai temple in the Mekong Delta.

People of other religions also have places of worship in Vietnam. This is the Christian St Joseph's Cathedral in Hanoi.

Sacred head

Buddhists believe that the head is the highest or most **sacred** point on the body, and the feet are considered the lowest and dirtiest point. You should never touch someone on the head or point your toes at people, as it is very insulting! When visiting a Buddhist pagoda, you should take off your shoes.

sacred something that is respected or worshipped

Getting around

Motorbike madness

There are over 10 million motorbikes in Vietnam! In the north, a Russian-made motorbike, called a Minsk, is common. The bike, which sounds like a chainsaw, is good for tackling rough roads and hilly areas.

After the excitement of Ho Chi Minh City, you decide to explore further. There are many different ways of travelling round Vietnam, including train, car, bus, or motorbike.

Plenty of tour companies offer bus trips, where you buy one ticket and hop on and off the buses throughout the country. The buses can be hot, though, and the ride can be very bumpy, as many roads are in poor condition, with lots of potholes. Travelling by car isn't much better and as there is a lot of traffic, people tend to honk their horns a lot!

If you want to travel around Vietnam quickly you will need to fly. There are 24 airports in Vietnam, so this isn't a problem, but it can be an expensive way to see the country.

In Vietnam, people use motorbikes as a quick and easy way of travelling around the towns and cities.

WORD BANK sabotage deliberately damage something

Train travel

The Reunification Express is the most famous train in Vietnam. It travels 1,726 kilometres (1,073 miles) between Ho Chi Minh City and the capital, Hanoi. During the Vietnam War, trains could not make regular trips, as the north and south of the country were fighting each other. Soldiers would **sabotage** the line by carrying away big chunks of track during the night. In 1975, the rail link was re-established and became a symbol of the end of the Vietnam War and a **unified** country. This is where it got its name from.

The railway between Ho Chi Minh City and Hanoi was begun in 1899 and took 37 years to complete.

Speedy hydrofoils

In the north you can catch a Russian-built hydrofoil between Cat Ba Island and Haiphong. A hydrofoil is a boat with fins underneath, which lift the front of the boat out of the water so it can travel at faster speeds. The hydrofoils are almost three times quicker than a ferry!

Fast fact

It takes 24 hours by express train from Ho Chi Minh City to Hanoi. Other trains are much slower, and the journey can take between 30 and 40 hours!

Country life

You are here!

Mekong Delta

You catch a bus down to the Mekong Delta. Bright, green **rice paddies** are everywhere – which isn't surprising as almost 40 percent of the country's rice comes from here! A small wooden boat waits for you by the edge of a river. You head off down a maze of waterways and canals towards the Cai Be floating market, where lots of stall-holders gather in boats on the Tien River. On the way, you see small stilt houses, fruit orchards, and lots of fish farms.

A large population

The Mekong Delta covers around 60,000 square kilometres (23,166 square miles), and is close to the size of the Hawaiian Islands. Even though it is relatively small, around 17 million people live here, more than fourteen times the population of Hawaii!

Most of Vietnam's food comes from the Mekong Delta – including 24 percent of the country's pork, 30 percent of poultry, and 24 percent of eggs.

14   **WORD BANK**   rice paddy wet land where rice is grown

Markets on the water

At the market, hundreds of colourful long, thin sampan boats dot the water. Each boat has a pole at the front, which displays the goods for sale. The traders sell all kinds of fresh produce, including fish, rice, fruit, and vegetables. There are floating petrol stations, floating schools, and even floating hairdressers!

Almost 80 percent of Vietnam's population lives in the countryside. Many people work in the paddy fields, growing rice.

Hungry?

The average Vietnamese person eats around 13 kilograms (29 pounds) of rice a year. This makes Vietnam the fifth-biggest rice-eating country in the world! Most rice comes from wet-rice paddies, which means it grows in flooded fields rather than on dry land.

15

Fishing

Along the coastline, fish are an important source of food and income. There are thousands of motorized fishing boats in Vietnam. These boats travel down rivers and into the ocean to catch fish in gigantic nets. Often fishermen will live or sleep on their boats.

Country homes

You organize a home-stay on the river in a small wooden house, which is built on stilts. You take off your shoes before entering the house – this is considered polite in Vietnam. Seven people live in the house, including the parents, two children, grandparents, and an aunt. Often in Vietnam the immediate and extended family will all live under one roof.

Many houses are built on stilts so that when river water rises, the houses won't be flooded.

WORD BANK   delicacy type of speciality meal from a particular culture, country, or place

A Vietnamese feast

For dinner your hosts cook up elephant-ear fish, a local **delicacy**, served with rice. Now you're full and sleepy so you pop into your bed. The mattress is very hard and covered by a mosquito net. You make sure the net covers every inch as you don't want to be bitten by a mosquito – they carry **malaria** and can be deadly. You are awoken early by the children leaving the house. Their father is taking them to school by boat.

In Vietnam's mountainous areas, rice terraces are built on the slopes to stop the water running off the mountain. The steps catch the water, which is necessary for the rice to grow.

Farm life

Farm life involves hard work for the whole family. Growing rice needs everyone to take part – from children to grandparents. They all work long hours. There is also the cooking and cleaning to be done. Other chores include going to the market and taking care of the water buffaloes, ducks, and pigs.

malaria infectious disease spread by mosquitoes

City life

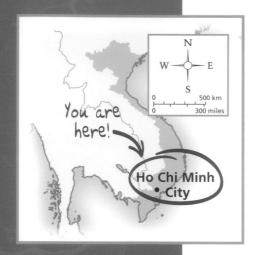

You are here! → Ho Chi Minh City

After relaxing in the countryside you feel like a change of pace, so you jump on a bus back to Ho Chi Minh City. When you get there you find the city streets are complete chaos. There is traffic everywhere – even on the footpaths. A motorbike zips by, carrying a pig strapped in a basket and three passengers!

A motorbike taxi pulls up and offers you a ride. The driver introduces himself as Nguyen Huy. He explains that Nguyen (pronounced Nwee-en) is the most popular family name in Vietnam – rather like Smith in English.

Cyclos and motorbike taxis

A slow way to get around the cities is by cyclo – a three-wheeled cycle, with a big passenger seat. However, most city people need to travel around quickly and prefer to jump on a motorbike taxi.

There are around 2,000 cyclos in Ho Chi Minh City alone!
►

Fast fact
Ho Chi Minh City is named after the former leader of North Vietnam. Before 1975, the city was called Saigon.

WORD BANK French Colonial from a time when France ruled Vietnam

Market places

You drive straight to the centre of town, to the bustling Ben Thanh Market. This huge market is housed in a beautiful **French Colonial** building, which was built in 1914. There are hundreds of stalls, selling everything from fish to watches. Lots of people are haggling over the prices. You buy a *non la*, a cone-shaped hat. The hat is made of palm leaves and will be useful for providing shade from the sun and shelter from the rain.

The Reunification Palace was once known as Independence Palace, but is now a symbol of a **unified** Vietnam.

The Reunification Palace

The Reunification Palace in Ho Chi Minh City was once the symbol of the South Vietnamese Government. Its basement contains a network of tunnels so people could quickly escape during the Vietnam War.

Ho Chi Minh City facts

Population: 6 million
Area: 2,094 square kilometres (809 square miles)
Major Industries: food-processing, machine-building, fishing, textiles

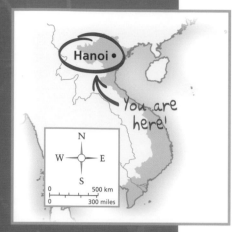

Exploring Hanoi

You have seen some incredible sights in the south of Vietnam, so now it's time to discover the north of the country. You catch a flight to Hanoi, Vietnam's capital. When you get off the plane you notice that it is a lot cooler and everything is a bit slower than in Ho Chi Minh City. A *Xe om*, motorbike taxi, offers you a lift to your hotel. *Om* means to cuddle – so you hop on the back and hold on tight as the driver weaves through the streets.

The magic sword

You ride past Hoan Kiem Lake, one of Hanoi's most important sites. Local legend tells that hundreds of years ago, King Le Loi stopped a Chinese invasion with a magical sword which had been lent to him by the King of the Sea. After the battle, an enormous turtle rose from the lake and demanded the sword back, and it was returned to the waters.

Street names

Around 500 years ago, Hanoi's streets were named according to what goods were sold there. Each street begins with the word *Hang*, which means "merchandise". *Hang Ma* is one such street, where paper is sold.

Motorbikes drive through a street market in the capital Hanoi.

WORD BANK   corpse dead body of a human being
embalming process used to preserve bodies

Tube houses

You spot some funny tube houses – that are only 2 metres (6.6 feet) wide. Many of them have a shop at the front and a house at the back. You wonder how they fit everything in, but then you notice that some of them stretch back more than 50 metres (164 feet)! Hundreds of years ago Hanoi's houses were taxed by their width, so to avoid big tax bills people built long, narrow houses!

The mausoleum that contains the body of Vietnam's former leader, Ho Chi Minh.
▼

Spooky!

At Ho Chi Minh's **mausoleum** you can see the preserved **corpse** of Vietnam's former leader, Ho Chi Minh, who died in 1969. The mausoleum is closed for three months every year, during which time the corpse is flown to Russia for **embalming**.

Hanoi facts
*Area: 921 square kilometres
(572 square miles)
Population: 3.1 million
Major Industries: machinery,
computers, electronics,
metallic products, textiles*

mausoleum large, grand tomb, usually built for an important person

21

Entertainment

It's a cold, misty morning so you go for a walk to warm up. A passing jogger tells you to head for Hoan Kiem Lake, where most people in Hanoi go for their morning work-out. When you get there you see lots of people exercising, doing tai chi – a graceful, slow exercise, which originated in China

Other people are playing badminton and some are out jogging – this place is fitness central! Vietnamese people are very active; they also enjoy other recreational activities like going to the cinema and **karaoke**.

▲ People enjoy the peace around Hoan Kiem Lake in Hanoi.

Cinema

After work many people take time out by going to a *rap* – the cinema. Cinemas can be found in all major cities across the country. English movies are sometimes dubbed over by one Vietnamese voice-over, who will vary their voice for both male and female, and the young and old parts!

WORD BANK karaoke singing popular songs to recorded music

Watching soap operas is also a popular pastime. As well as soap operas from their own country, the Vietnamese enjoy those from China and Korea.

Kicking around

Vietnamese people love to kick around a shuttlecock (*Da cau*). Shuttlecock is considered a national sport and is played by kicking a shuttlecock over a net. Feet, chest, and even the head can be used to volley the shuttlecock – but it must not touch the hands. Shuttlecocks were originally made out of coins and feathers bound together, but these days they are usually made out of plastic and feathers.

Football

Vietnam is football-mad! During major tournaments, like the World Cup, the whole country stays up late at night to watch the games. Lots of men get together on Saturday nights to watch soccer on television at home and in the cafés.

People gather to watch a game of badminton taking place in a local park in Hanoi.

Vietnamese theatre

You decide to go and see a *mua roi nuoc* performance – a water-puppet show. Water puppets perform in a pool, on the water's surface. The puppeteers stand waist deep in the water, but are hidden by a screen or a stage. The performances usually tell stories from Vietnamese folklore, history, or day-to-day life in **rural** Vietnam. Stories of harvests, fishing, and festivals will often feature alongside fire-breathing dragons, buffaloes, and farmers. Often the puppets fight and get their heads chopped off!

Pop stars

Vietnamese people love to sing – they even have television shows that teach people how to do it! Vietnam has a large pop-music industry and prefers Vietnamese stars to those from overseas. Some big Vietnamese pop stars are Thanh Lam, Hong Nhung, and My Linh.

A water puppet show in Ho Chi Minh City. Water puppetry is believed to have originated in the Red River Delta in the 10th century.

WORD BANK

lute stringed instrument shaped like half a pear
percussion instruments that are hit, shaken, or scraped to make a noise

A Vietnamese orchestra and singers help tell the story. At dramatic moments, cymbals and drums are clanged together. Watch out if you sit in the front seat, as you could get wet!

Traditional music

Traditional music is very popular in Vietnam. There are over 50 Vietnamese musical instruments, such as **percussion** instruments, like the *Trong dong* (copper drums) and *Cong chieng* (gongs). Stringed instruments are also popular, like the *Dan nguyet* (a moon-shaped **lute**) and the *Dan nhi* (a violin).

Vietnamese crafts

- Lacquerware (*son mai*) – layers of **resin** spread on top of each other, often with egg-shells added for decoration, to create beautiful lacquerware objects like vases, chopsticks, or bowls.

- Silk painting – since the 13th century, Vietnamese artists have been painting beautiful pictures on silk.

This man is making a lacquerware panel in a factory in Ho Chi Minh City.

➤

resin material that forms a hard layer to protect a surface

Festivals and holidays

Vietnamese people enjoy life and love spending time with family and friends throughout the year. However, nothing compares to the big party atmosphere during Tet – the Vietnamese New Year. Tet is celebrated in late January or early February, and is the country's biggest holiday.

Before Tet, the markets get very busy and people decorate their homes with blossoming trees and *Cao doi* – red paper with good-luck messages. There are dragon parades every night and dancing in the streets in the lead up to this exciting holiday.

Market stalls sell lavish decorations in red and gold, ready for the Tet celebrations.

Fast fact

At Tet, people try to wear something red, as it is believed to be a lucky colour.

New Year countdown

On *Giao Thua*, New Year's Eve, shops shut early and everyone heads home to start celebrating with their close family and friends. The whole country waits up until midnight, to welcome the New Year. When the clock strikes twelve, every person in Vietnam turns a year older, and says "Chuc mong nam moi" – Happy New Year! On *Mong Mot Tet*, New Year's Day, everyone dresses in their best clothes. Houses are decorated with flowers and everyone gets together and eats delicious foods like tasty *mut* (fruit candies) and *Banh chung* (sticky rice cake). Children receive red envelopes from elder family members and friends. Inside the envelope is *Tien lixi*, lucky money. It isn't real money, but is thought to bring good fortune.

The Vietnamese believe that freeing birds at Tet will prevent bad luck in the coming year.

Day of the Wandering Souls

In August, *Trung Nguyen* is celebrated – the Day of the Wandering Souls. This is the second-largest festival of the year, and people make offerings of food and gifts to the wandering souls of the forgotten dead.

27

People & culture

An old woman is standing on the corner laughing. You notice that her teeth are pitch black and she has red, round circles on her forehead! Black teeth were traditionally considered beautiful, as was a big messy hairdo like a rooster. These days, though, most women prefer to have sparkling white teeth and neat hairstyles.

Traditional medicine

The marks on the woman's forehead are from cupping, *giac* – a traditional medical treatment. A small heated glass is applied to the skin. As the hot air inside the cup cools, it contracts and creates a **vacuum**. This vacuum is believed to draw out illness or bad energy. The glasses are placed where the pain or illness is felt, such as on the forehead to treat a headache, or a person's back to treat a backache. Traditional medicine like this is very popular in Vietnam.

The Vietnamese language

In Vietnamese, the same word can have several different meanings, depending on how it is pronounced. The word *ma* has eight different meanings – ghost, cheek, but, which, who, tomb, horse, or rice seedling!

Women sell traditional medicines, including herbs and spices, by the side of the road in Vietnam.

Another treatment is coining, *cao gio*, where coins are rubbed across the skin, causing scratches. These are believed to release illness from the body and restore balance. One of the best-known treatments is acupuncture, where thin steel needles are inserted into specific points. It is believed that each of these points has an effect on a particular organ in the body.

A patient receives acupuncture, which is believed to cure illness by restoring balance to the body.

Location, location!

Vietnamese people believe it is important to pick the perfect site for a new home – as the wrong location can bring very bad luck! This ancient art of selecting a lucky location is called geomancy (*phong thuy*).

Survival tip

People's names in Vietnam are said with the family name first, the middle name next, and then the given name. They are referred to by their given name, though, so Nguyen Huy would be addressed as Mr Huy.

Love Market

Many people come to Sapa to see the Weekend Market, where different people gather from the surrounding hills to sell their handicrafts. Historically, the market was known as the "love market", because people from nearby villages would come to meet with their sweethearts here.

The Hmong

You head to Sapa, a small town in the misty, chilly mountains. The landscape is stunning, with towering mountains dotted with little huts and giant rice terraces. You see some people from the Black Hmong community, dressed in black clothes, and wearing big silver necklaces around their necks. They are selling some crafts from their village, so you buy a woven blanket to keep warm.

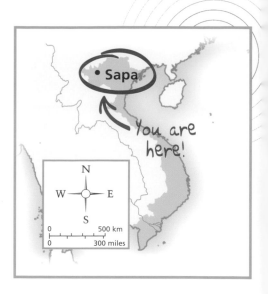

A young Black Hmong boy stands by a water pipe system in **rural** Vietnam.
➤

WORD BANK   dowry present, such as land, money, or goods, given to a new husband by the bride's family

Ethnic groups

Hmong people tend to live in higher mountainous areas, and farm crops like corn and rice. The farmers often rely on "slash-and-burn" agriculture, which means they cut down trees and burn them to make the soil more **fertile**, before the crops are planted. There are many different Hmong groups in Vietnam, including the Black Hmong, Red Hmong, White Hmong, and Flower Hmong. You can tell the different groups apart by the clothes they wear. The Hmong are just one of over 54 **ethnic groups** in Vietnam. The largest groups are the Tay, Thai, and Muong.

Smaller families

Families are much smaller now than they were 50 years ago. Because Vietnam has such a large population, the Government encourages people to have no more than two children.

In the mountain villages, women are skilled weavers and make items such as colourful shawls and bags to sell at the local markets.

Minority groups

- The Tay is the largest group and they usually live in villages named after the mountain, field, or river nearby.

- The Thai are fantastic embroiderers, and when girls become teenagers, they make blankets for their **dowries**.

- The Muong are known for their excellent musical talents, and play instruments like the pan-pipes, flute, and drums.

fertile suitable for growing crops

Street kitchens

All this exploring has made you hungry. Around Sapa there are many different restaurants to choose from. You see lots of people eating at street kitchens – small restaurants specializing in one or two meals. Most street restaurants have outside seating, where adults sit on very small chairs and share their meals.

It is fine to slurp your soup in Vietnam as it shows you appreciate your food.

Young people enjoy a meal outside a restaurant in Hanoi.

Unlucky chopsticks

Leaving chopsticks standing upright in a bowl of rice is thought to be very bad luck! It only happens at funerals, when a bowl of food, with chopsticks, is offered to the dead person.

WORD BANK fermented broken down by chemicals, often by leaving to stand

Favourite foods

You look over a menu at one of the bigger restaurants. On offer are *nem rán* (spring rolls), *bún thang* (noodles with pork, eggs, chicken, and shrimp), and *pho* (soup). You choose *pho*, one of Vietnam's most popular dishes. On the table is a bottle of **fermented** fish sauce, a popular seasoning served with nearly every meal. The salty sauce tastes good, but it smells really strong! It is so strong that even Vietnam Airlines has banned it from their aeroplanes!

French Food

France once ruled Vietnam, and there are some reminders of this time. There are cake shops all over Vietnam where you can buy French-style baguettes and special pastries. The Vietnamese have also adopted other French foods like paté, ice-cream, and coffee.

Soup is a favourite dish in Vietnam. It is even eaten for breakfast!

Cats and tigers

Vietnamese people believe that women should eat small amounts, like cats, and men should eat lots of food, like tigers.

Nature & climate

Dragon descending

Halong means "dragon descending". According to local legend, Halong Bay was created when the gods sent a dragon to frighten invaders. The mighty creature fell to Earth and flicked its large tail through the waters, splitting mountains, churning up rocks, and creating thousands of islands.

Vietnam is home to hundreds of amazing plant and animal species, including rare animals like the Asian elephant, the rhinoceros, tigers, leopards, bears, gibbons, and crocodiles. You catch a bus to Halong Bay to learn more about Vietnam's landscape and wildlife.

The ocean comes into view and your jaw drops open – it's beautiful! There are over 3,000 stunning **limestone** islands poking out of the clear blue water. You travel to a port in Halong city and arrange to take a ride on a junk – an old, Chinese-style yacht.

Vietnamese people believe that the Tarasque, a type of monster, lives in Halong Bay. You are more likely to see crabs, birds, and fish, though.

▼

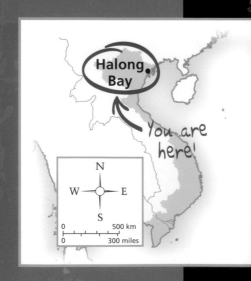

Halong Bay

You are here!

N
W — E
S

0   500 km
0   300 miles

WORD BANK   limestone soft white rock
mangroves tropical trees or shrubs that grow in marshes or shallow water

National parks

There are 87 national parks in Vietnam, including historical sites and nature reserves. Cuc Phuong National Park, established in 1962, was the country's first national park. Two **Neolithic** tombs, believed to be over 7,000 years old, have been found here.

Phong Nha-Ke Bang National Park is also a fascinating place to visit. It is the second-largest limestone area in the world, and has many caves and underground rivers. It is believed that the rocky formations in the park started forming around 400 million years ago!

Mist hangs over the forests that cover the mountains in Hoang Lien National Park.

Cat Ba National Park

Cat Ba National Park in Halong Bay is set in wonderful natural surroundings. There are beaches, reefs, jungles, lakes, swamp-lands, and **mangroves**. The park is also home to a range of animals, such as leaf monkeys and wild pigs.

Survival tip

The sack tree, Antiarus Toxicaria, has a poisonous **sap** *that people once used to make deadly arrows.*

Neolithic dating from the Stone Age, around 10,000 BC
sap liquid from a plant

Climate

Vietnam's diverse geography – which includes mountains, valleys, and beaches – means there are very different weather patterns.

Vietnam has a topsy-turvy **climate**. When one part is cold, another part is usually warm. There are two different climate zones – the north zone and the south zone. It is always warm in the south! In the north it can get pretty cold in the winter – sometimes down to 0°C (32°F). Snow is rare, but occasionally falls in the higher mountainous areas of the north, such as Sapa.

Natural beauty

There are thousands of natural wonders in Vietnam – caves, mountains, beaches, and waterfalls. Over 200 rivers flow from the mountains to the sea. The country has a 3,444-kilometre (2,140-mile) coastline.

Vietnam is affected by **monsoons**, which blow in from other countries and create different climate conditions across the country.

WORD BANK

climate typical weather conditions in an area
monsoon season of winds, which are usually accompanied by heavy rains

Seasons

The south has two seasons: the rainy season (from May until October), and the dry season (from November until April). The north has four seasons: spring (from February until April), summer (from May until July), autumn (from August until October), and winter (from November until January).

The mighty Mekong

The Mekong River is over 4,000 kilometres (2,485 miles) long. It starts in the Tibetan **Plateau,** at the top of China, and runs through five countries before it plunges into Vietnam's Mekong Delta, and empties into the South China Sea.

The Mekong is the twelfth-longest river in the world.

plateau area of high, flat land

A bit of history

Uncle Ho

Ho Chi Minh was born in 1890. He was nicknamed Uncle Ho (*Bac Ho*). He was president of North Vietnam from 1954 to 1969, and led his army to victory against the French at Dien Bien Phu. He died before the end of the Vietnam War.

You make your way to Dien Bien Phu and visit the museum. You see that France ruled over Vietnam from the mid-19th century. Vietnam was part of France's empire. In 1954, a major battle took place in Dien Bien Phu between the French and the Viet Minh (Vietnamese **Communist** Forces). The Viet Minh surrounded the town, digging tunnels and trenches, until the French surrendered.

The battle not only ended French rule, but also led to the country being split into two parts – the Communist-ruled north and a **republic** in the south. The split was supposed to be temporary, until elections could be held to find a new leader for the country. Instead it led to the Vietnam War.

French soldiers stand in trenches during the Battle of Dien Bien Phu in 1954.

WORD BANK   republic form of government where there is usually a president

The Vietnam War

In 1957, the North and South of Vietnam began fighting each other in what became known as the Vietnam War. As the war continued, other countries joined in, including the United States and Australia, who supported South Vietnam. In 1973, the United States pulled its troops out, but the war continued without them until 1975, when South Vietnam surrendered. It is estimated that between 3.2 and 5 million people died in the war, most of them Vietnamese.

The Cu Chi Tunnels were equipped with kitchens, hospitals, and weapon factories – all underground!

Cu Chi tunnels

The Cu Chi tunnels lie to the north-west of Ho Chi Minh City. They originally spanned more than 250 kilometres (155 miles), and stretched all the way to the Cambodian border! The tunnels were used by North Vietnamese forces during the Vietnam War.

Fast fact

What we know as the Vietnam War is called the American War by the Vietnamese.

It's ancient history

People were probably living in the region of Vietnam thousands of years ago. Officially, though, the history of the country began 4,000 years ago, when it was founded by the Hung kings. In those days, it was called Van Lang.

An ancient city

You want to find out more about Vietnam's history, so you travel to Hue, a city set on the banks of the Perfume River.

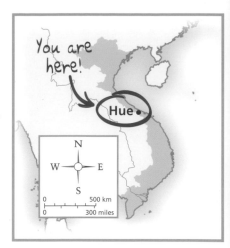

This was the capital of Vietnam from 1744, when the Nguyen lords, a line of royal rulers, controlled all of southern Vietnam from the city. Hue is like one big museum and has lots of old buildings. The **Citadel** is a fort, surrounded by a big moat. Work began on the Citadel in 1805, during the reign of Emperor Gia Long. It took more than 20,000 workers to complete it! Inside the Citadel walls is the ruined Imperial City. The Citadel was badly damaged in 1968, during a period in the Vietnam War called the Tet Offensive.

Buddhist nuns in the ancient Imperial City in Hue.

WORD BANK   abolish get rid of or do away with something
citadel fortress built to protect a town

The Tet Offensive

In 1968, North and South Vietnam agreed to stop fighting so people could celebrate Tet. On 30-31 January, though, North Vietnamese forces launced a series of surprise attacks on cities in South Vietnam, known as the Tet Offensive. The South Vietnamese and US forces fought back with a massive bombing campaign that forced the North Vietnamese to retreat.

The Last Emperor

Bao Dai (which means "Keeper of Greatness"), was only twelve years old when he became emperor in 1926. He stood down in 1945. In the 1950s Vietnam decided to **abolish** the **monarchy**. Bao Dai was Vietnam's last emperor.

Many buildings in Hue were damaged during the Vietnam War. This colourful gate leading to the Imperial City has since been rebuilt.

Bao Dai was the last emperor of Vietnam.

monarchy form of rule where a king, queen, or emperor is head of state

Stay or go?

You have seen some wonderful things in Vietnam, but there is still so much you could do. You pull out your map and look at some of the other places you can visit. Should you stay or go?

Time for a dip

You haven't spent much time exploring Vietnam's beaches – and there are hundreds of them! Ha Tien, near the Cambodian border has crystal-clear waters and shady, sandy beaches. Nearby are several caves, which are fun to explore. Nha Trang is Vietnam's most popular beach resort town. You can also enjoy water-sports like water-skiing, snorkelling, scuba diving, and riding jet skis. Beautiful Phu Quoc Island is also known as the Emerald Island because of its great beauty and palm-lined beaches.

Craft villages

Bat Trang village, near Hanoi, is a well-known pottery village, where villagers make bricks and ceramic items. Here you can see a vase being sculpted or bricks being fired in kilns behind people's houses. Another interesting village nearby is Van Phuc, where you can see silk being made and woven.

Men enjoy fishing from colourfully decorated boats in Ha Tien.

The best of the rest

- Dambri Waterfall drops over 90 metres (295 feet), making it the tallest waterfall in Vietnam.
- Phong Nha Cave is Vietnam's largest cave, formed about 250 million years ago!
- At 3,143 metres (10,311 feet), Mount Fansipan is the country's highest mountain and considered the rooftop of Vietnam.
- Lake Ba Be is the largest natural lake in Vietnam and is 8 kilometres (5 miles) long and up to 30.5 metres (100 feet) deep.
- Beautiful Phu Quoc is the largest island in Vietnam, covering an area of 573 square kilometres (221 square miles).

A man pushes his cart down a street in the tourist village of Hoi An.
▼

Express tailors

The old medieval port town of Hoi An is known for its beautiful old buildings. In recent years, it has become famous for its express tailors, who can whip up a dress, suit, and other clothing overnight.

Find out more

Destination Detectives can find out more about Vietnam by using the books and looking at the websites listed below.

World Wide Web

If you want to find out more about Vietnam, you can search the Internet using keywords such as these:

• Vietnam
• Hanoi
• Ho Chi Minh City

You can also find your own keywords by using headings or words from this book. Try using a search directory such as www.google.co.uk.

The Vietnamese Embassy

The Vietnamese Embassy in your own country has lots of information about Vietnam. You can find out about the different states, the best times to visit, special events, and all about Vietnamese culture. The website for the Vietnamese embassy is: www.vietnam.embassyhomepage.com

Further reading

Ask About Asia: Vietnam by Judith Simpson (Mason Crest, 2002)

Children of the Dragon: Selected Tales from Vietnam by Sherry Garland, Trina Schart Hyman (Harcourt Publishers, 2001)

Children of Vietnam by Marybeth Lorbiecki and Paul P. Rome (Carol Rhoda Books, 1997)

Countries of the World: Vietnam by Michael Dahl (Bridgestone Books, 1998)

Culture in Vietnam by Melanie Guile (Raintree, 2005)

Enchantment of the World: Vietnam by Terri Willis (Children's Press, 2002)

Onion Tears by Diana Kidd (Harper Trophy, 1993)

Taking Your Camera to Vietnam by Ted Park (Raintree, 2001)

The Culture: Vietnam by Bobbie Kalman (Crabtree Publishing, 2002)

The Land I Lost: Adventures of a Boy in Vietnam by Huynh Quang Nhuong (Harper Trophy, 1986)

The Lotus Seed by Sherry Garland (Voyager Books, 1997)

WORD BANK   colony area under the rule of another country
merchants professional traders who sell goods

Timeline

3000–1000 BC
People are known to be living in the Red River Delta.

207 BC
Kingdom of Nam Viet is established by a Chinese general.

AD 939
The country gains independence from the Chinese emperors and the first independent state is established.

1428
The Chinese are driven out of the area.

1600s
French **merchants** and **missionaries** arrive in the region and encourage the French government to set up a **colony**.

1802
Prince Nguyen Anh unites all the different northern, central, and southern regions into one country and calls it Vietnam.

1887
Vietnam is officially a French colony.

1930
Ho Chi Minh starts the Indochinese **Communist** Party.

1932
Bao Dai, the last emperor, begins his reign as a twelve-year-old child.

1941
Ho Chi Minh forms the Viet Minh communist forces and arranges for them to fight for Vietnam's independence.

1945
Ho Chi Minh declares Vietnam's independence and an end to **French colonial** rule. The French refuse to accept this and reoccupy Indochina (Cambodia, Vietnam and Laos) as a colony.

1946
France bombs Haiphong Harbour. This marks the beginning of an eight-year struggle between France and the Viet Minh.

1954
Vietnam defeats the French at Dien Bien Phu. Vietnam is split into two parts – the Communist-ruled north and a **republic** in the south.

1957
Fighting begins between the north and the south of Vietnam.

1959
The Ho Chi Minh trail is built. The Vietnam War begins.

1965
The United States sends combat troops to Vietnam. Bombing in North Vietnam begins.

1968
Tet offensive begins.

1972
"Christmas bombing" of Hanoi and Haiphong.

1973
The United States signs a peace agreement with North Vietnam. The war continues though.

1975
South Vietnam surrenders.

1976
North and South Vietnam are united under Communist leadership.

1995
Relationship with the United States is re-established.

2005
Prime minister Phan Van Khai becomes the first Vietnamese leader to visit the United States in over 30 years.

---

missionaries people who go to another country to do religious work

45

Vietnam – facts & figures

The Vietnamese flag consists of a yellow star in the centre of a red background. The five points on the star symbolize the people of Vietnam: farmers, workers, intellectuals, youth and soldiers. The background red stands for revolution and bloodshed.

People and places

- Vietnam is one of the most densely populated countries in the world, with around 230 people per square kilometre (600 per square mile). It has the tenth-highest population density in the world!
- The official, local name for Vietnam is Cong Hoa Xa Hoi Chu Nghia Viet Nam, which is shortened to Viet Nam.
- Life expectancy: Men – 67.8 years; women – 73.6 years.

Technology

- Mobile phones: 2.8 million.
- Internet users: 3.5 million.
- The country code for Vietnamese websites is .vn.

Trade and industry

- Main industries: food processing, garments, shoes, machine-building, mining, cement, chemical fertilizers, glass, tyres, oil, coal, steel, paper.
- Main exports: crude oil, marine products, rice, coffee, rubber, tea, garments, shoes.
- Vietnam is the second-biggest producer of rice in the world.
- Vietnam is the world's biggest producer of robusta bean, the coffee bean used for instant coffee.

Glossary

abolish get rid of or do away with something

citadel fortress built to protect a town

climate typical weather conditions in an area

colony area under the rule of another country

Communism belief that all the wealth created by industry should be shared amongst everyone in society

corpse dead body of a human being

delicacy type of speciality meal from a particular culture, country, or place

dowry present, such as land, money, or goods, given to a new husband by the bride's family

embalming process used to preserve bodies

ethnic group people who share a culture or nationality

fermented broken down by chemicals, often by leaving to stand

fertile suitable for growing crops

French Colonial from a time when France ruled Vietnam

karaoke singing popular songs to recorded music

limestone soft white rock

lunar calendar calendar based on the cycle of the moon

lute stringed instrument shaped like half a pear

malaria infectious disease spread by mosquitoes

mangroves tropical trees or shrubs that grow in marshes or shallow water

mausoleum large, grand tomb, usually built for an important person

merchants professional traders who sell goods

missionaries people who go to another country to do religious work

monarchy form of rule where a king, queen, or emperor is head of state

monsoon season of winds, which are usually accompanied by heavy rains

Neolithic dating from the Stone Age, around 10,000 BC

pagoda T-shaped building, with a bell-tower, used for worship

percussion instruments that are hit, shaken, or scraped to make a noise

plateau area of high, flat land

reincarnation belief that a person will be reborn after they die

republic form of government where there is usually a president

resin material that forms a hard layer to protect a surface

rice paddy wet land where rice is grown

rural relating to the countryside

sabotage deliberately damage something

sacred something that is respected or worshipped

sap liquid from a plant

unified joined together politically

vacuum when air has been removed from a space creating a suction effect

Index

Destination Detectives

China

North America

Europe

Asia

Africa

CHINA

South America

Australasia

Ali Brownlie Bojang

www.raintreepublishers.co.uk

Visit our website to find out more information about **Raintree** books.

To order:
☎ Phone 44 (0) 1865 888112
▤ Send a fax to 44 (0) 1865 314091
▣ Visit the Raintree Bookshop at **www.raintreepublishers.co.uk** to browse our catalogue and order online.

First published in Great Britain by Raintree,
Halley Court, Jordan Hill, Oxford OX2 8EJ,
Part of Harcourt Education.
Raintree is a registered trademark of
Harcourt Education Ltd.

Produced for Raintree Publishers by Discovery Books Ltd
Editorial: Kathryn Walker, Sonya Newland,
Melanie Waldron and Lucy Beevor
Design: Gary Frost, and Rob Norridge
Picture Research: Amy Sparks
Production: Chloe Bloom
Originated by Modern Age
Printed and bound in Hong Kong

10 digit ISBN 1 4062 0718 7 (hardback)
13 digit ISBN 978-1-4062-0718-7
10 9 8 7 6 5 4 3 2 1
11 10 09 08 07

10 digit ISBN 1 4062 0725 X (paperback)
13 digit ISBN 978-1-4062-0725-5
10 9 8 7 6 5 4 3 2 1
11 10 09 08 07

British Library Cataloguing in Publication Data
Brownlie Bojang, Ali, 1949–
    China. - Differentiated ed. - (Destination Detective)
    1. China - Geography - Juvenile literature 2. China -
    Social life and customs - 21st century - Juvenile literature
    3. China - Civilisation - Juvenile literature
    I. Title
    951'.06

This levelled text is a version of *Freestyle:
Destination Detectives: China*. Produced for Raintree by
White-Thomson Publishing Ltd.

Acknowledgements

The Art Archive pp. 17 (William Sewell); Corbis pp.
9 (Reuters), 10 (Keren Su), 13 (Xinhua), 15t (Royal Ontario
Museum), 28 (Ron Watts), 29 (Keren Su), 33 (Chi Haifeng/
Xinhua), 38 (Michael S. Yamashita), 38–39 (Vince Streano);
Photolibrary pp. 4–5 (Pacific Stock), 7 (IFA-Bilderteam
Gmbh), 10–11 (Panorama Stock Photo), 12 (Panorama Stock
Photo), 15b (Pacific Stock), 19 (Index Stock Imagery), 20–21
(Panorama Stock Photo), 21 (Panorama Stock Photo), 24
(Panorama Stock Photo), 27 (Panorama Stock Photo), 31
(Panorama Stock Photo), 34 (Botanica), 35 (Pacific Stock),
37, 40 (Daniel Cox), 41 (IFA-Bilderteam Gmbh), 42
(Panorama Stock Photo); TopFoto pp. 16 (Nathan Strange/
uppa.co.uk), 25 (Image Works); WTPix pp. 5t, 5m, 5b, 6, 8,
14, 18, 22, 23l, 26t, 26b, 30, 32, 36, 43.

Cover photograph of lion dance reproduced with permission
of Panorama Stock Photo Co., Ltd/OSF/Photolibrary.

Thanks to Luo Jailing and Simon Scoones.

Every effort has been made to contact copyright
holders of any material reproduced in this book.
Any omissions will be rectified in subsequent
printings if notice is given to the publishers.

The paper used to print this book comes from
sustainable resources.